THE LAW OF
REACTION

How Everything Happens

Layout & Design: Creative Culture
Cover Art: Apple Desktop Photo
Author Photo: Antonia Partridge

Published by Snowbird Books

ISBN: 978-0-9735918-3-5

Night Owl appears courtesy of WikiCommons.

All names have been changed.

Disclaimer: *The Law of Reaction* is not a cure, but simply an attempt to describe *How Everything Happens*. Almost too simple for both the author and publisher to understand, neither can be held liable for any use or misuse of the information contained within these pages ☯ please enjoy responsibly.

Email your praise and flame to:

oliverlukedelorie@gmail.com

TABLE OF CONTENTS

✷ THIS BOOK IS UNIQUE

✷ THERE IS ONLY LOVE

✷ TRUE FRIENDSHIP

✿ HOMEWARD BOUND

✿ WONDERFUL WORK

✿ FABULOUS FUN

✜ Absolute Abundance

✜ World Peace

✜ Resources

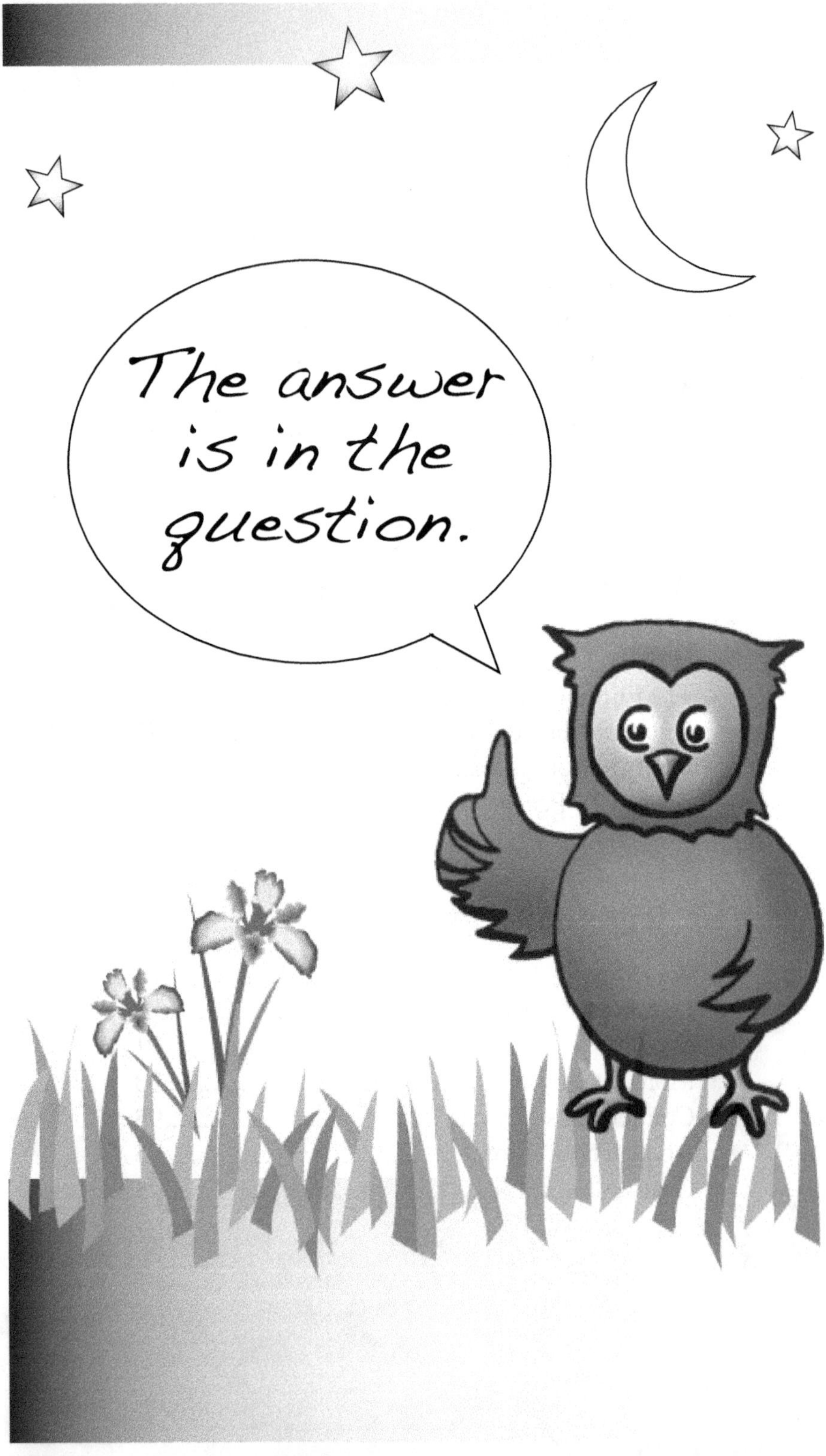
The answer is in the question.

❦ This Book Is Unique

This book is intentionally short and sweet, because our time is more valuable than anything.

The Law of Reaction will answer every question, because *The Law of Reaction* is how everything happens. Whether we know it or not, like it or not, or want it or not, like attracts like in the circle of life, while opposites are busy attracting each other too. This book attempts to uncover this universal truth.

Every second of every day we are either moving towards or away from the energy personified as god, goddess, allah, jah, buddha or krishna. Some describe this energy field as love, the force, consciousness, zen, zero, the creative source or (my favorite) unity.

Everything originates in unity; everything begins as one, connected to everyone and everything. We are born into duality and life is an endless struggle to find and maintain the perpetual balancing act of nature.

We are tricked into believing the illusion that duality is reality, but the truth is that unity is reality.

By celebrating inevitable opposites, instead of denying they exist, we find everything we seek.

Reggae legend Bob Marley reminded us how *the things we refuse are the things we should use*. What are we refusing to see, to hear, to touch, to taste?

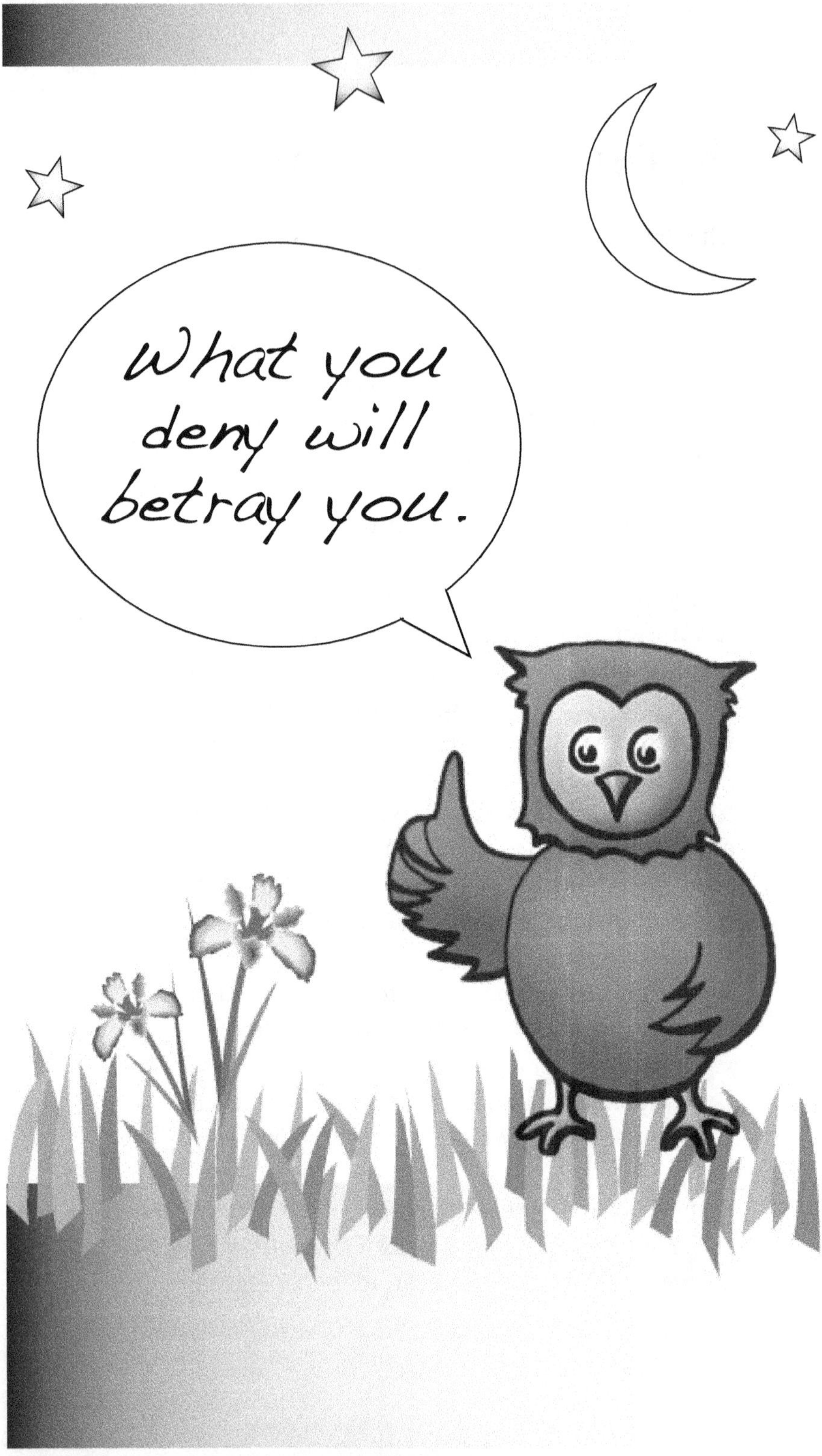
What you deny will betray you.

DUALITY

Duality means two. Everything appearing separate is not. There are two sides to every story, remember?

Duality is the constant friction of particles and people attempting to find connection and lasting harmony and is what keeps us spinning around the sun, walking, talking, kissing and shopping.

Duality exists in every religion, thought, science, art, object and action. Nothing exists without its opposite: Yin and yang, heaven and hell, light and dark, yes and no, ebb and flow, above and below.

We naturally seek balance, consciously or not, yet find balance either one step ahead, or one step behind. Duality is the puppeteer pulling our strings.

We cannot have one thing without the other, and will create problems to fill the gaps of ones we solve.

The deeper we breathe in, the deeper we breathe out, and the faster we drive, the faster we wear out our brake pads. My friend Scott says *by doing nothing, we do nothing wrong*.

Why do we judge ourselves, our friends and our families? When we stop denying the existence and potential for opposite possibilities in ourselves and others, forgiveness inevitably leads to our salvation and wholeness. This is what we are after anyway.

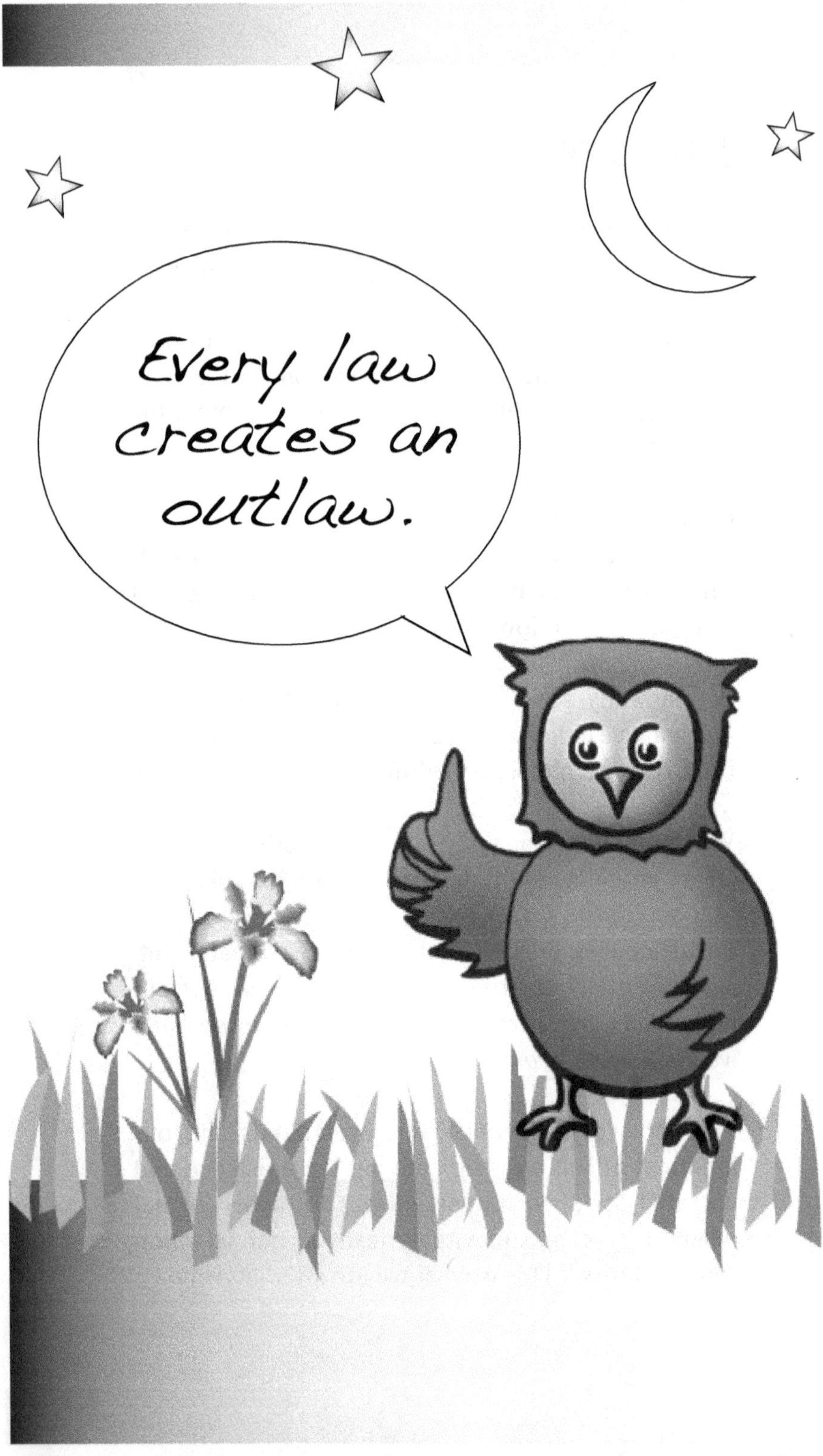
Every law creates an outlaw.

PARADOX

Einstein said to *look deep into nature and we will understand everything better.*

How can something be one thing, yet another, all at the same time? Paradox explains the conflict we see, hear and feel everyday. Nothing is as it seems, no matter what we think it means.

So how do we become something we are not, get something we do not have, or get somewhere we want to go, as quickly as possible, while paradox is behind everything?

If we want something, the best way to get it is by paradoxically not wanting it. Seem strange? Try it.

Why do we ignore our lives are full of opposites and oxymorons; jumbo shrimp, objective opinions, same difference, original copies and military intelligence?

In developed countries with an abundance of resources we expect people to be happier or more fulfilled, yet the paradox is they are not.

We place more value on what is expensive and less value on what costs little. Looking at life in reverse will always reveal what is real.

Sheryl Crow flips the switch with her lyrics: *it's not getting what you want; it's wanting what you got.*

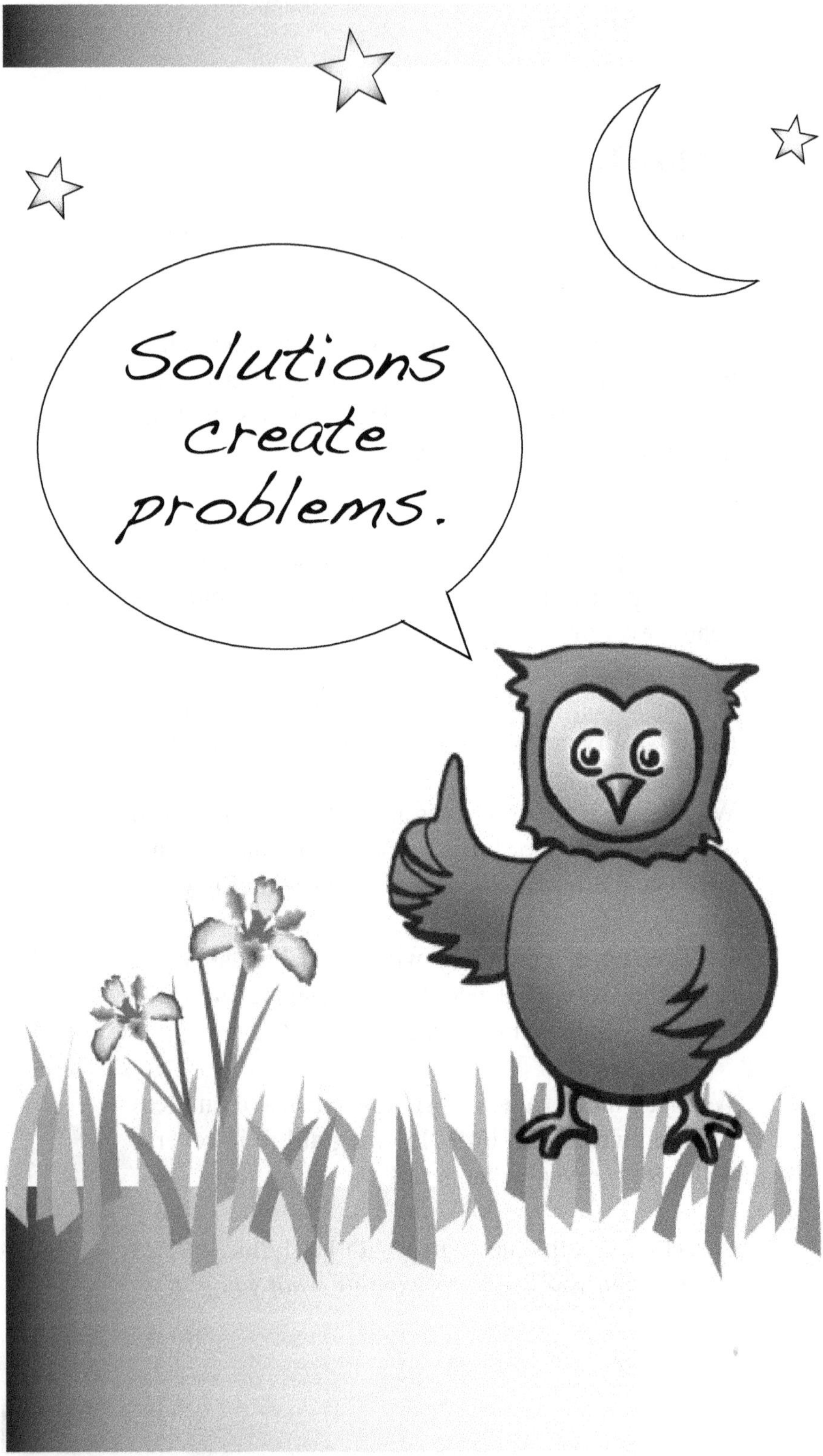
Solutions create problems.

CAUSALITY

Causality is a word expressing the science behind *The Law of Reaction*; how every action has an equal and opposite reaction.

The strength and quantity of every single reaction is equal to, and in direct proportion to, the strength and quantity of what originally caused the action.

Everything we see in the physical world has qualities both exactly resembling, and in complete opposition to, the thoughts we think and the actions we take.

We do not consciously do anything without knowing the reasons why, so we must go looking for a cause.

The cause behind an effect may not be obvious, which leads us to ask: what is the cause to this effect?

When we hit our heads against a brick wall, the brick wall is hitting us back. Permanent equilibrium is obvious only when we see how we are the cause of every effect in our lives.

We take responsibility, because *it is only with the heart that one can see rightly; what is most important is invisible to the eye*, says the Little Prince.

Everything is connected; nothing is separate. When we remove the mask and toss the disguise, we begin to see as if we had new eyes.

POLARITY

Batteries have two terminals; one positive and one negative. Everything under the sun runs on electricity and work only when these two currents, plus and minus, come together to produce power.

My friend Adriane says *as long as we live, we will be harmonizing polarity*, the ultimate goal of the universe, and the secret to *The Law of Reaction*.

But sometimes polarity works in our favor and sometimes not. Both conduits and circuit breakers, the last thing we want is a power outage.

We are made of electrical energy, both positive and negative, both at the same time. Esther Hicks says *there is no exception. We are source energy.*

For something to exist, its opposite must exist also. Polarity is another key to how everything happens.

There are two directions to the flow of energy. Left and right, back and forth, up and down, in and out.

The way we direct our energy determines our well-being, so harmonizing our polarity for maximum effect is the best way to keep our lives in check.

We swim upstream until we either become the creative source itself, or resign as general managers of the universe. Two steps forward, one step back.

ENTROPY

Entropy is the opposing force working against us and everything we do, destroying what we create in an attempt to find a sense of balance.

In the process of creating either order or disorder, Entropy has some help from its friends friction and gravity, who get involved and either slow down or speed up our process.

The more we take action, the more mixed results we get, whether we are building a house or tearing it down to the ground.

Notice the energy we expend at work and at home lasts only as long as we expend it?

If we throw a pile of bricks off a truck, chaos takes over and organizes our man-made building blocks into a mess we clean up before the boss gets back.

The amount of entropy decreases only to the degree we increase the amount energy we expend, which also has opposite effects. Nothing is constant or static.

When we are not paying attention, the world around us is busy falling apart, whether we like it or not.

Like a shovel left out in the rain, entropy ultimately takes over and turns our neglected toys and tools to rust. The tide ebbs and flows. This is how it goes.

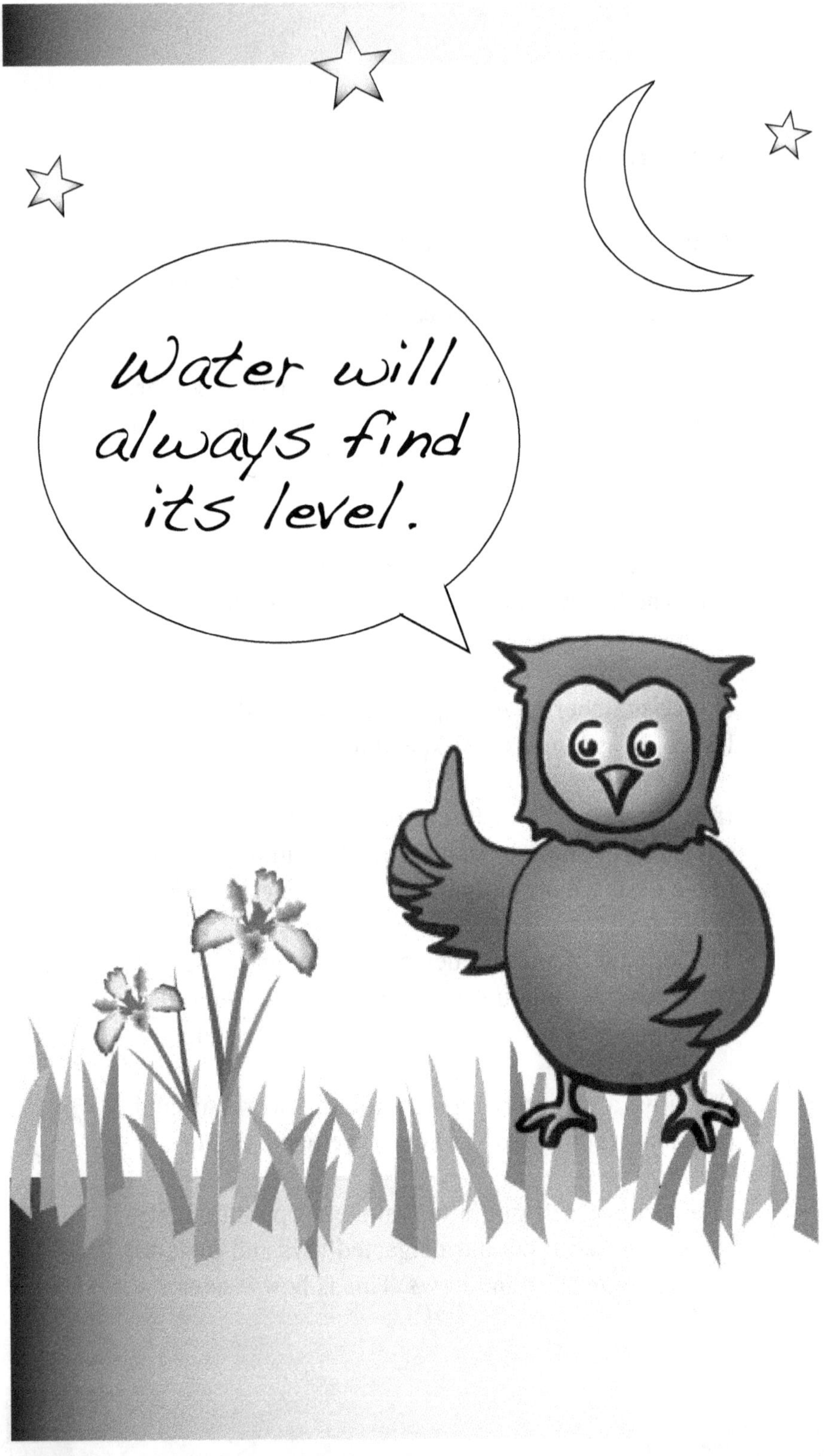
Water will always find its level.

IRONY

Irony is when the opposite of what we expect to happen happens. How often does this happen? When does it not happen?

There is an agenda larger and greater than ours waiting to pull an ace from its sleeve. *If something can go wrong it will*, says Ed Murphy.

Ronald Reagan was struck by a bullet that ricocheted off the very car intended to protect him.

Ku Klux Klan members regularly light themselves on fire, divorced people insist on giving marriage advice, and bald people have hair everywhere else.

Teachers pity slow learners, who inevitably turn out to be the highest achievers. And we think winning the lottery will answer our prayers, but it will not.

Authors send their books to dozens of publishers only to receive rejection letters. As soon as they give up, their books are published and become best-sellers.

We see NASA scientists regularly using toys to illustrate their points, fitness centers using escalators instead of stairs, and pink lung-shaped ashtrays.

The irony is, the more we try to be safe, the more vulnerable we are. The Wizard of Oz was nothing but a scrawny little dude hiding behind a curtain.

HYPOCRISY

No doubt we often find ourselves leaning to one side or another when it comes to making a choice.

We are bound to be affected if we say the opposite of what we think and do the opposite of what we want to do, but it seems we do this more often than not.

Hypocrisy is inevitable. Nothing can be maintained indefinitely when we are governed by constant flux.

We do what we say no matter what.

Living with integrity is an immense challenge; it means walking our talk, long after the thrill is gone.

We find answers hiding in the last place we would ever look. How would our worst enemy solve this problem?

We must look where we have not.

There is no such thing as left or right, winning or losing, right or wrong. Every opinion is subjective.

The more we are out-of-sync with our thoughts, words and actions, the more we become disconnected from what matters and separate ourselves from harmony.

Life is like an orange; by paradoxically loosening our grip we squeeze more juice out of it.

🌀 There Is Only Love

What is love? What does it feel like? What does it look like? What does it sound like? We have probably experienced love if we have ever known:

- Happiness
- Joy
- Appreciation
- Respect
- Abundance

We experience love every day, in one form or another, but may not know it. There are pros and cons to everything. If we look we find them. We see what we want to see and see what we believe. What do we see? What do we believe?

How To Find Love

We can find love in one of two ways. Either by giving it or taking it away. Our way is but one way.

Expecting love to be returned from the people or places we give our love to in the first place can be disappointing, so we let go of our expectations.

Love expresses itself in the most creative ways. Take a thimble or a bucket to the ocean of love; how much we ask for is irrelevant, love is aloof like a butterfly. Chase it and it flies away, but sit still and love lands gently on our shoulders.

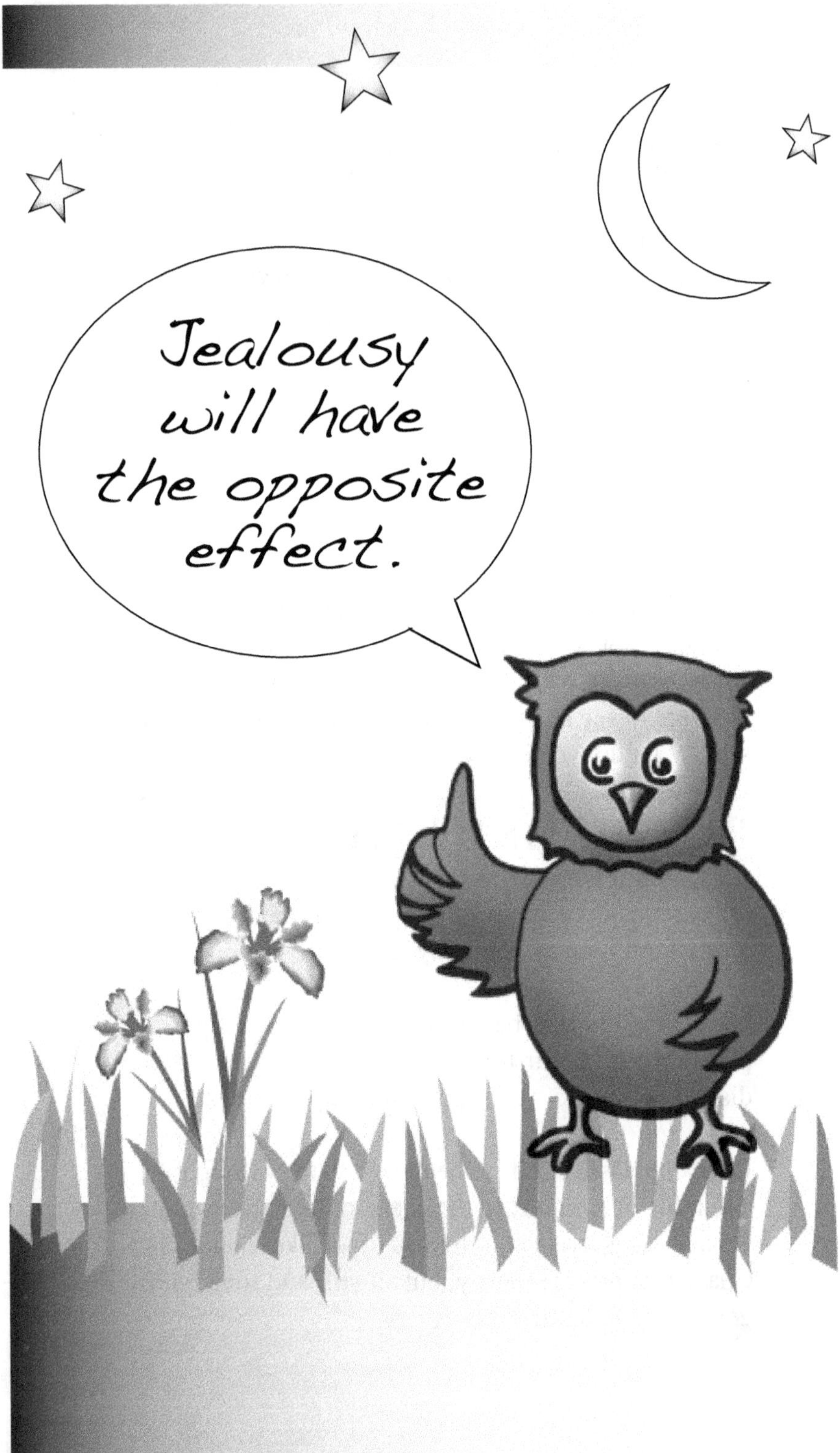
Jealousy will have the opposite effect.

HOW TO LOSE LOVE

Blinding ourselves to love by chasing it, keeping it all to ourselves or disrespecting it is harder than allowing it to find its own way, which is the point.

This goes for anything we are hell-bent on getting in our lives. If we bulldoze everything in our path, life gets ugly. But maybe we have to go to extremes; only we can decide. If we want different results, we have the ability to choose an alternative route.

THE FLIP SIDE TO LOVE

When we have experienced one side of the coin, we can experience the other, shifting our brains into low gear to see our cups half full, instead of half empty.

We meditate, exercise, chant, drum, play music or sports, focus on breath, write and speak affirmations, and giggle at how stressed we get about everything.

When we feel strongly about someone or something, watch out, because love has a bite that stings.

There is opposite potential in each and every person and situation we meet. Hills need valleys and the other way around. There is no love without hate.

Love is more fun when we share it, especially when we know we stand on common ground with each other. For each of us it is the same, now and always.

QUESTIONS FOR REFLECTION

- Have you ever been in love?
- Have you ever been in hate?
- What was the difference?
- How did you know which was which?

Love in all its billions of forms is both a blessing and a curse. Forget this and we are destined to remember.

MY STORY

After years of taking love for granted, I got dumped by my girlfriend, got fired from my job, went on welfare, broke my ankle, actually burned my musical instruments to keep warm (!) scrounged through trash cans for leftovers, skipped out on bills, and eventually ended up living in my Volkswagen van.

I had either turned off my emotions like a robot or gushed with tears, over-compensating for what I did not know.

Every tragedy was a blessing in disguise; I knew the harder it seemed, the more I would have to yield.

When I took a closer look, I saw how every problem had a solution, and how every solution had a problem. Suddenly, opposites appeared to hold the key, so I started owning all my negativity and it was like changing channels on the TV.

The more I learned to face my denied shadow side, the more I was able to embrace, if not celebrate, the dark, ugly, jealous, nasty, hungry, angry ogre inside me. Needless to say, I began to feel free.

It did not matter if I did not understand something, like it, or want it. What I was denying was betraying me, my family, my friends and my dreams.

Love, without the experience of simultaneously hating the same people, places and things, was hollow and shallow to me.

Once I could appreciate the feelings in opposition to what I really wanted to feel, I began to love in a way that seems to span beyond time and space.

The simple solution? I found love hiding in the last place I ever thought to look: inside my own heart.

3 STEPS TO LOVE

1. Love Is All Around You

2. Breathe It Like Air

3. You Will See It Everywhere

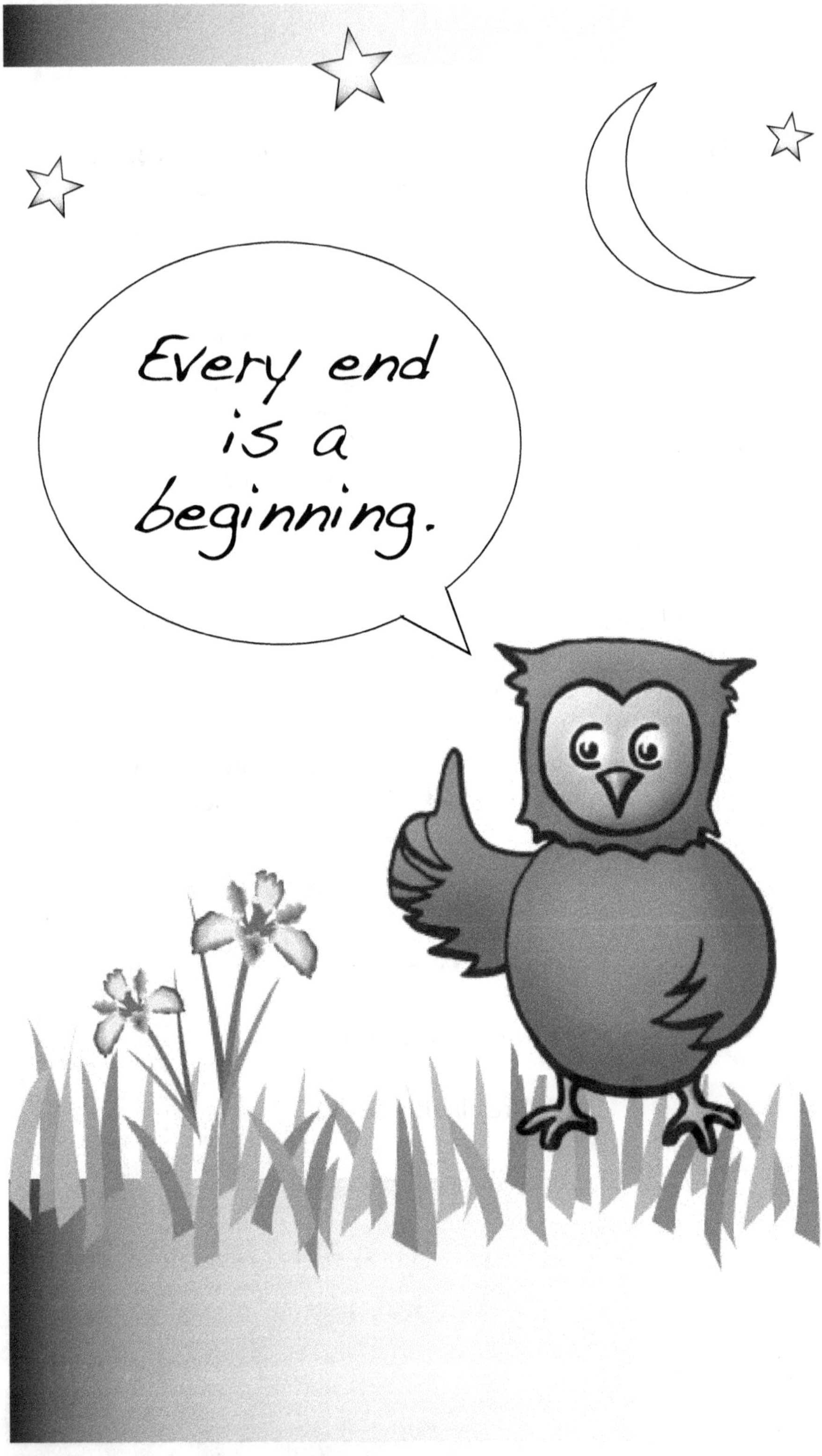
Every end is a beginning.

✺ True Friendship

Some people say friends are worth more than gold.
Yes or no? Most people choose friends over money
or possessions, but where does that get them?

True friends:

- Listen without judging
- Drop everything to help us
- Make us feel comfortable without even trying

Wayne Dyer says *our friends are gods way of
apologizing for our families.*

How To Find Friends

The more we allow ourselves to be who we truly are
and go our own way, the more we attract people just
like us, after sifting through the sludge of course.

Why worry about all the oddities cluttering around
in our heads, keeping us from venturing into new
territory? Where do the greatest gifts inevitably lie?

If we have always wanted to do something, we do it.
The odds are definitely in our favor. The house wins,
but are we not the house? We have to bet big to win
big. Playing small serves no one.

We make friends who like us for who we are, love
what we do, and who respect our inner truth.

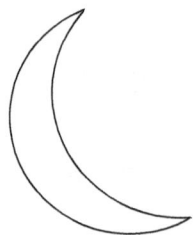

HOW TO LOSE FRIENDS

By giving our fears not only more power than they deserve, but also more importance than our happiness, we will be 80 years old and wonder what-the-hell happened.

What stops us from taking more risks? What stops us from laughing more? What stops us from sharing our lives with those we care about?

We know how much it sucks being lonely, but trying to be everything to everyone will only end badly, like everything else that is out of harmony, but in it.

THE FLIP SIDE TO FRIENDSHIP

When we give and give and give without getting, we converse with the people we give our love, time, money and energy to, and ask if they want to continue the relationship. We must love and let go of the past.

We can always find new friends to replace the ones we lose, because the more people we meet, the more we see one of three possibilities:

- We are appreciated and accepted
- We are not appreciated and accepted
- We do not even register on their radar

Remembering this before we venture out into the big, cold world, or the small, warm one, will help.

QUESTIONS FOR REFLECTION

- Do you have any friends?
- How do you know they are your friends?
- How does having friends make you feel?
- How does not having friends make you feel?
- What is the difference?
- Can you be alone and enjoy it?

JEREMY'S STORY

When I met Jeremy he was great at avoiding people. He had lost his parents in a car wreck, was an only child, and had lived with his aunt until he chose to support himself with his large inheritance.

Not surprisingly, Jeremy felt abandoned. He trusted no one and kept to himself, playing video games and ordering pizzas when he was not sleeping. He rarely left his apartment.

Jeremy had finished his game and was in a good mood when the pizza arrived. Turned out he and the delivery driver graduated together; instant recognition.

Poking his head into Jeremy's apartment, his new friend noticed the game console, made a comment, and they chatted for hours.

He was stuck near the end of the game, and asked Jeremy for some advice. Noticing the open window, and having seen only closed doors since his parents

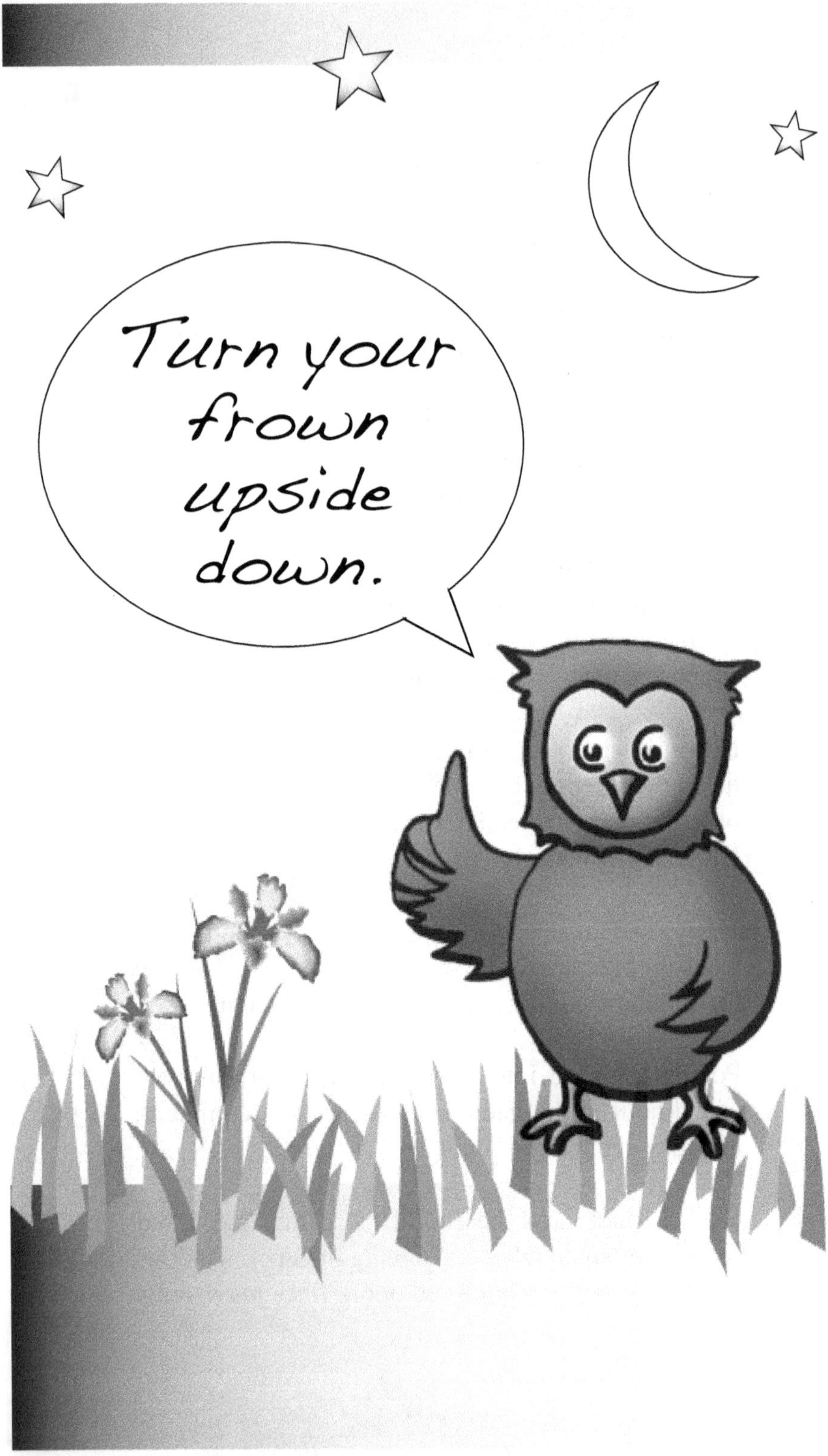
Turn your frown upside down.

died, Jeremy came out of his shell, shed his old skin, and has been dating his friend's sister for a year.

All it took was one small step. Just one.

When the opportunity presented itself, Jeremy's intuition whispered in his inner ear, encouraging him to leap, even though he could not see a safety net to catch him if he fell.

But his desire for change was stronger than his fear, so the net appeared. But paradoxically, he did not even need it.

His excitement enriched his life because he allowed himself to take a chance and try something new.

It all began with a pepperoni pizza. Simple or what?

3 STEPS TO FRIENDSHIP

1. Do You Want Friends Or Gold?

2. What Is More Important?

3. You Are Free To Choose

❂ Homeward Bound

We need roots to grow fruit. Our well-being depends on being grounded, otherwise we may feel:

- Sad
- Lost
- Confused
- Angry
- Hungry

How To Find A Home

Home is wherever we are. If we have a spouse, partner, kids, pets or plants and are not appreciating them like they ought to be, how about it?

If we have an empty fridge, recycling piling up, and there is nothing on TV, we buy some food we like, get our deposit back and rent a comedy. When we love the pavement cracks, they love us back.

How To Lose A Home

Ignore our home and all its contents, breathing and not, and we wake up one day without them. Then what do we do? Where do we go? What happens to our kids, pets and plants?

Homes wither with neglect if we stay away too long. Do we want a happy home or not? Time to decide.

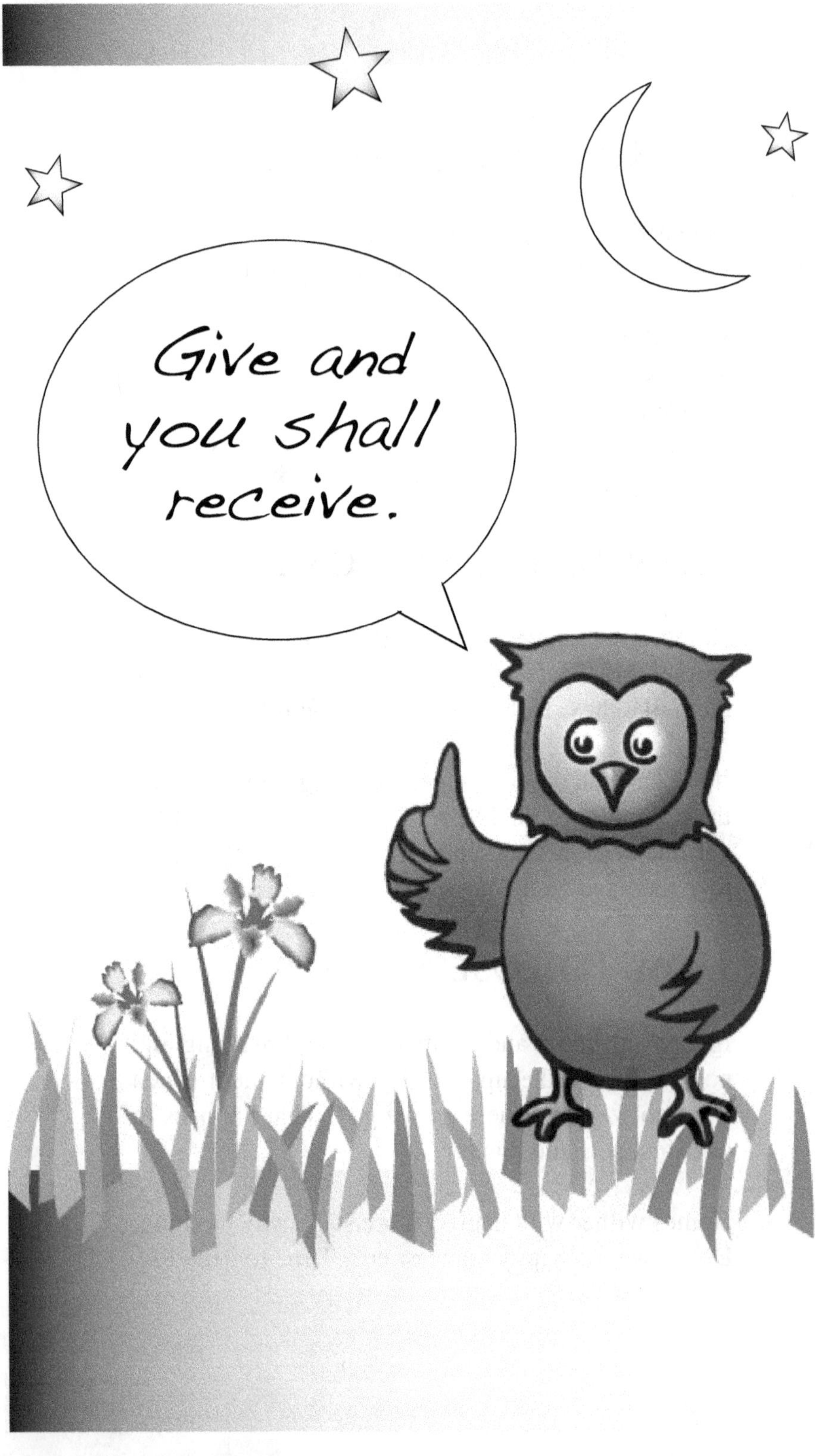
Give and you shall receive.

Wondering if the grass is greener on the other side of the fence leaves us feeling dissatisfied with everything. We will not feel at home anywhere, actual roof over our heads or not.

THE FLIP SIDE TO HOME

When we look for something, we tend to only see what we want to see, no matter what is going on.

What we focus on expands, so focusing on finding joy at home will either reward us with more joy, or provide a chance for us to celebrate a challenge.

We go with the flow and see the blessings in disguise nudging us home, regardless of what we think is happening. Regardless of the push and pull, our world is our oyster to shuck as we please.

QUESTIONS FOR REFLECTION

- What is it like to be home?
- What is it like when you are not there?
- Where is your home?
- How do you know you are there?

SARAH'S STORY

I met a single mother named Sarah. Thankfully, Sarah's mother lived down the street and looked after her grandchild while Sarah was busy with this and

Create a void and it will be filled.

that. She went out with her friends nightly, drinking regularly until dawn and was as worse from the wear as her jean jacket.

Sarah was lost in a fog of foolish folly, selfish and self-absorbed and had more boyfriends than she could remember. Were they really unmemorable?

It took a serious reaction to her son's flu shot to sober her up, having to wait at his bedside for him to return. Why did it take a wake-up call to wake her up?

Sarah has since started her own cake decorating business and is so focused on her little boy, her mother has to bribe Sarah to spend time with her grandson.

Why do we want to be old when we are young, and young when we are old? By avoiding pain and seeking pleasure, we miss out on the magic and mud of life.

3 STEPS TO HOME

1. Your Heart Is There

2. You Cannot Live Without Your Heart

3. Go And Get It

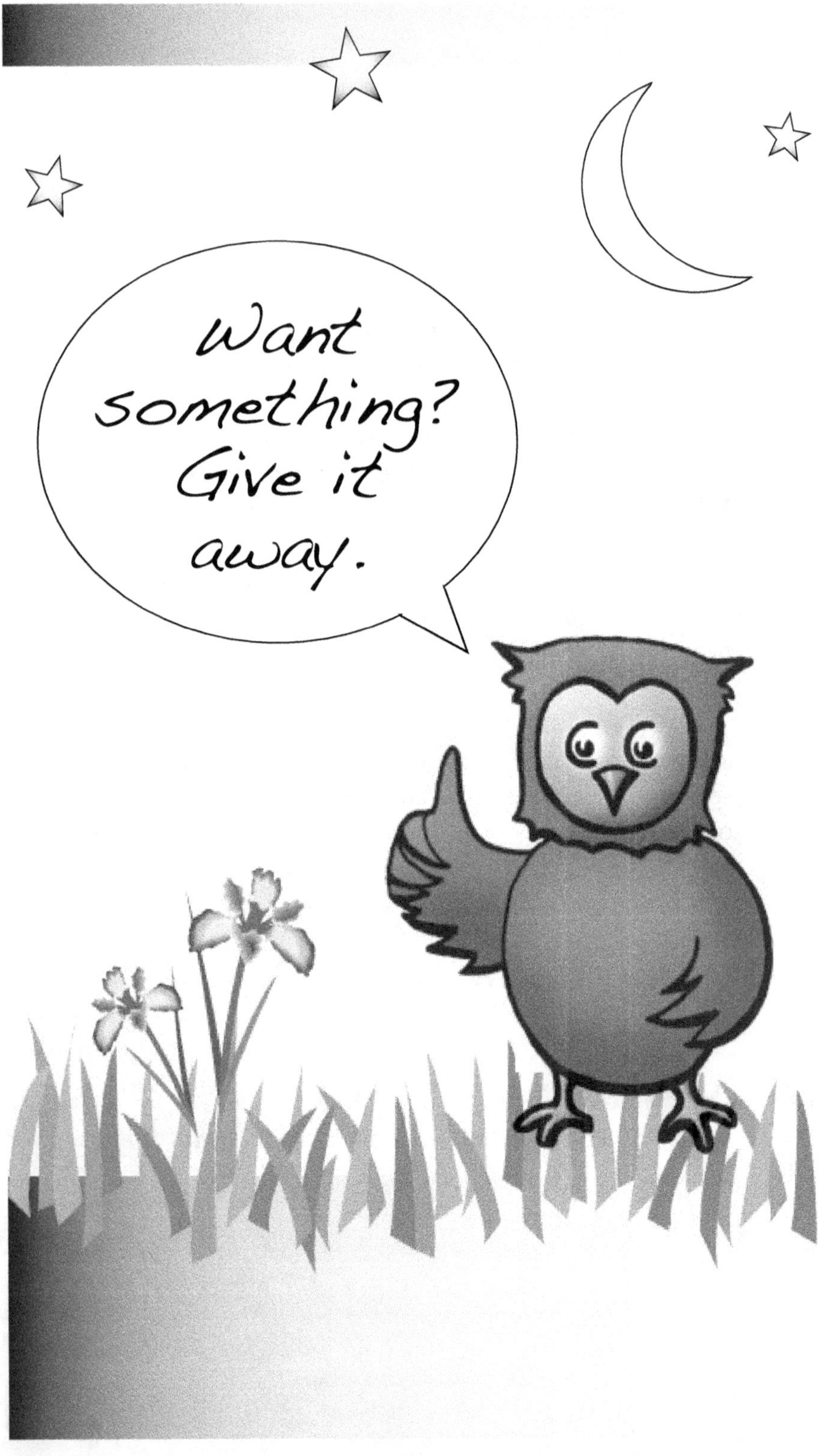
Want something? Give it away.

🌀 WONDERFUL WORK

Working for our own benefit and the benefit of others is a big part of our lives, but if like most people we work at least forty hours a week, fifty weeks a year, we are unsuited for how we spend our time if:

- We dread the sound of our alarm clock
- We feel like a hamster on a treadmill
- We complain about our boss or coworkers
- We find ways to slack off at work

If any of the above applies, we are lucky if we have been laid off, fired, or have quit our jobs to find more satisfying ways of providing for ourselves and our loved ones, even if it was challenging at first.

Is it in our best interest to trade our time for bits of paper that decline in value every day?

Our lives are short and our lives are long. If life is short we start living. If life is long, rowing our own boat is more satisfying. Results require effort.

What turns us on? Can we turn a passion or hobby into some food, clothing, rent, car repairs, dance lessons, furniture, coaching or childcare?

We can trade for what we want, and forget about the printed pieces of tree pulp seducing us like a drug. The best things in life are not things; we know this truth deep down in the basement of our souls.

How To Find Work

To find meaningful work and right livelihood we make a list of what we like to do. What brings us a sense of accomplishment? From this list, we pick one pursuit and pursue it one hour a day, then two, then four, then six, facing our fear of success.

We slowly increase the amount of work we do for ourselves, our friends and our families, and slowly decrease the amount of work we do solely for a paycheck, some adrenaline and a lot of stress.

We see results within weeks, and have more energy to keep going. All the resources we need show up and help us succeed. Belief is our best guarantee.

If we need a computer, we go and get it. If we need money, we watch as it weaves its way into our lives like magic. Once we earn money, it comes easily.

But if we only work for money, that is all we get. Until we can love being poor, we cannot be rich; our fear of poverty will haunt us, even when our bathtub is filled with moolah instead of water.

How To Lose Work

Avoid anything and we are doomed to see it everywhere we look. We can lose work by working too hard and/or taking it too seriously, so we follow our bliss, whatever we believe that is.

The Flip Side To Work

Our glass is either half full or half empty, so if we want to keep working at our jobs, we start appreciating the good things about it. There has to be at least one.

Maybe our coworkers make us laugh. Maybe we get health benefits for us and our family and maybe we value this over our pointless dissatisfaction.

We turn problems into a business, because changing jobs only gets us more of the same. Even when we are self-employed or retired, we have to find balance in what we do. If we volunteer, play sports, go fishing, entertain or teach people, finding or creating meaning in all we do can be simple.

Questions For Reflection

- What would you do if you could do anything?
- What and/or who are you working for?
- How would you like to spend your time?

Bailey's Story

Bailey worked way more than I did, forty hours more, at a job with financial rewards, but not much else.

Her life lacked creativity and inspiration, and being on auto-pilot all day long kept her from realizing her burning desire to be a ballet dancer; she knew all it

would take was to focus less on impressing her boss, and more on impressing herself.

Bailey signed up for her first dance class after some *Creative Sensation*[1] exercises, sensing how excited and motivated she would feel doing what she had always wanted to. She made time to fulfill her dreams by facing and embracing her fears of being too old and out of shape.

When she realized these limiting beliefs no longer served their intended purpose, getting her back into balance, she let them go. Her sense of accomplishment was in direct proportion to the difficulty of the challenge she faced, like every possibility, everywhere, always.

Bailey told herself *yes* more times than she told herself *no*. When we do this too, we make our dreams come true. There is no limit to what we can do.

3 STEPS THAT WORK

1. Do What You Love To Do

2. You Will Hate It Too

3. This Is Bliss

✺ FABULOUS FUN

No doubt about it: fun is fun. We have experienced fun in our lives at one time or another if we:

- Laughed at a joke
- Liked how we felt doing anything
- Ate something that tasted good
- Tried something new and enjoyed it
- Created beauty and believed in it

Even if the last time we enjoyed ourselves was at our best friend's 10th birthday party, all hope is not lost.

All we have to do is go look in the mirror and laugh at how seriously we take everything.

Laugh at how frustrated we get at our partners, the traffic, our kids, our friends, our parents, our teachers, the neighbors, the war or whatever.

Laughing at ourselves is a great way to find fun in any situation, no matter how grim it seems. Celebrate at a funeral. Revel in life, instead of crying about it.

The last thing this person wants is for everyone to be miserable, unless they were miserable themselves, in which case a sense of humor will liven things up.

Ironic humor is lurking everywhere laughing behind our backs, so we lighten up and laugh back.

We all die one day, and will have nothing to worry about then, so why worry about it now? Why not celebrate the inevitable equal opposite to life.

When we at least welcome the thought, we find an enormous weight leaving our weary shoulders.

Ignore judgement. Why are we so concerned with what other people think of us? All they think about is what we think about them.

If someone says something is right or wrong or inappropriate, we question their motivations and ask if they have our best interests at heart. Misery, loneliness and fear have possessed them, like demons in search of sweet and sour souls worth savoring.

The goal of the universe is to eliminate the distance between two opposing forces. When we understand the finely-tuned flip side, there is fabulous fun to be had in foolishness.

We write and repeat the same tests over and over again, until we look and find the answer in the mirror. Until then, we just go around in circles.

We are made up of light beams and sound waves, yet are far from perfect. Such perfection does not, has not, and will not ever exist. Let go and let god.

We do not stop playing because we get old; we get old because we stop playing.

How To Find Fun

Finding fun is easy. Laughing is free and fun is everywhere. If we like food fights we have food fights; we just make sure the enemy either has a sense of humor, less tomatoes, or both.

If we like something, we do it, then find more opportunities to do it, or get so much opposition it fuels our inner fire. Playing with life is fun.

How To Lose Fun

Losing out on fun is easy too. All we have to do to take the fun out of something is be a stick-in-the-mud. If we are giving ourselves ulcers, losing money, or crying ourselves to sleep every night, we can take a break from our pity party before being forced to.

The more we go in one direction, the more we are shown another way. We pull out a periscope and have a look outside the rut, noticing an abundance of fantastic opportunities just itching to be scratched by our curiosity and passionate zest for life.

When our orchard yields more lemons than apples, we add sugar and make a thirst-quenching drink.

And when our trees inevitably bless us with more than we can use, we find a need and fill it. We might as well; whatever we resist persists.

THE FLIP SIDE TO FUN

There is a flip side to fun, like everything else. If we, heaven forbid, get addicted to fun, we are out of balance and best switch gears for a while.

Under-nourishment in the fun department means noticing the possibilities nudging us to get involved. We are our own best friends, so we start by inviting ourselves to the liveliest party in town.

If we like to be alone and keep to ourselves, stay home a lot, watch television all night and unconsciously fear people and our inner electricity, then all this fun popping up around us like popcorn might be uncomfortable.

But if we lash out at fun, we will only hurt ourselves when we mean to hurt others, for some twisted reason. Everything we do to someone, we do to ourselves, and everything we say, we say to ourselves.

QUESTIONS FOR REFLECTION

- What makes you laugh?
- What makes you cry?
- What makes you do both at the same time?

When we take the time to answer these questions, we might uncover a vein of gold we can mine to our heavy heart's content. Look up Julia Cameron for some encouragement in the creativity department.

Let us relinquish our stubborn pride and act like fools, especially if fear of folly scares us. Are we frightened by our invisible, meaningless, illusory reputation?

We are free to be whoever we want to be, free to think or say anything we choose. We are allowed to do whatever we want to. No one is stopping us.

ALEX'S STORY

Alex is a sous chef in a slow food restaurant I love. He was overweight and always said it was because he loved food and could not help but taste everything.

He worked tirelessly so he could excuse his ignorance and not have to make friends. He rarely cooked when he got home and he lived alone, so why should he?

When I pointed out how he ate fast food while promoting the slow food movement, we had a good laugh and Alex saw *The Law of Reaction* at work.

Alex asked and answered his own question. The cause was his pursuit of happiness, yet the effect was unhappiness. He wanted fun and freedom, but was doing everything to stop if from showing up; working too hard and eating too much.

A new server began working at his restaurant and immediately the two of them hit it off. This was Alex's chance to have some fun, but naturally he was scared, needing to be gentle with himself.

Issac Newton said *objects at rest tend to stay at rest, while objects in motion tend to stay in motion.*

Alex had always put his love, time, energy and resources into his work and into his stomach, and did not even know how to have fun.

But with a little coaching, he felt the fear and did it anyway, jumping headfirst into a relationship with his co-worker, deciding to trust his playful inner child.

Had he not taken a chance, he would likely have regretted not taking a chance. What is there to lose?

We are little kid animals masquerading as grown-up, civilized human beings, so we follow the silent voice guiding us with its sense of wonder and excitement.

No one will ever judge us more than we judge ourselves; we are our own worst enemies.

3 STEPS TO FUN

1. Do Something Silly

2. Laugh At Yourself

3. Do This Every Day

Treat other people like you were them.

❧ Absolute Abundance

Absolute abundance surrounds us now, even if it may not seem like it. We are surrounded with abundance if any of the following applies:

- We had breakfast or lunch or dinner today
- Someone else made it or bought it for us
- We are wearing clothes or shoes or socks
- We can express ourselves with language
- We have a vehicle, a bicycle, a bus pass or feet
- We have the eyes to read this book

We probably have some money in the bank, but think it is not enough. We own an iPod, home stereo, car stereo, discman, walkman, or all of the above, which allow us to enjoy the pleasures of music.

We likely have a roof over our heads and a bed to sleep in. With enough love, time, money and/or physical force, we can have any material comfort available, but is this really what we crave?

Sunshine, oxygen and water are signs we are provided for on the most basic levels, so we say goodbye to fear of survival. By enjoying and sharing what we are blessed with, we always have more than enough.

When we doubt we deserve abundance, we can use this doubt as confirmation we have always had what we needed, and we always will. We know it.

HOW TO FIND ABUNDANCE

We find abundance when we appreciate how everything comes into and our of form with zero effort. Nothing in nature strains to grow. We worry not, appreciate abundance and have it in abundance.

Enriching others is the only way to get rich, if that is what we desire. The more we serve, the more we deserve, getting what we give; no more and no less.

HOW TO LOSE ABUNDANCE

Losing abundance is easy. Complaining about how bad things are, about how little we have, and about how mean or angry or disappointed people are in us is a sure-fire way to get rid of what we want.

We are masters at repelling it, and whizzes at ignoring it. Love it or leave it. Use it or lose it. Get it?

Comparing ourselves against our neighbors is a great way to limit the flow of abundance; jealousy only turns off the tap. Why do we cut ourselves off from the limitless flow of love, time, money and energy?

Believe we are undeserving and our wish is our command. Instead, we pretend we are magnets and see ourselves united with our environment, without attachment, because getting attached to specific outcomes is what pulls the rug out from under us.

The Flip Side Of Abundance

We experience the flip side of abundance when we do not deeply appreciate what we already have.

When we spend money to make the world a better place, our supplies are replenished. When we spend time helping other people find pleasure in their lives, more time becomes available for us to spend however we see fit, though we are careful not to overdo it.

Prosper others and they prosper us. We give money to people and projects that inspire us, and vote!

We benefit family, friends and community with money or time. Regardless of the immediate results, inner peace has us in so much bliss we do not even notice our needs are met.

We choose to be content with less; wonderful material possessions can blind us to what is most important.

Questions For Reflection

- What are you appreciative of in your life?
- Why do you want more or less stuff?
- Have you ever had everything you needed?

Closing our eyes and expressing gratitude through any one, two, three, four or five of our senses, a few times a day, will invoke the gypsy curse: *May we get what we want.*

Mary's Story

My friend Mary was depressed, like many people, and birds of a feather flock together. She wondered why she found herself arguing with her parents over the amount of her allowance. Mary was thirty-five.

Her parents had given her everything. When she was sixteen, her father bought her a new car. When she was nineteen, her mother took her on a three-month tour of Europe, hoping to connect with her daughter in a way she had not before.

Mary had always drifted through life, accepting gifts and money in exchange for what she really wanted, but did not know how to get.

She had no idea what it felt like to be certain she would always be provided for, allowance or not.

Mary had not yet discovered how deserving she was of even the basic necessities of life.

She had relied on her parents to provide everything, and deep down she was scared to venture out on her own, secretly not trusting in absolute abundance, and fearing she would not enjoy it when it did show up.

After sleepless nights and endless fights, Mary's parents came to the conclusion they would stop supporting their daughter.

The time had come for Mary to get her act together.

She had six months. At first, she panicked, not knowing what to do. How would she live? Where would she live? What would she do? She was scared she would wither like a summer lily in winter.

Mary went on a bender and wrapped her car around a telephone pole. She woke up in the drunk tank the next morning, next to an old friend.

Old friend's boyfriend picked them up. He was a career counsellor at the college and suggested to Mary she come and see him the next day.

Mary is now completing a degree in business administration and plans on opening a health food store, following in her father's footsteps. All it took was a little belief in the nurturing nature of life.

3 STEPS TO ABUNDANCE

1. Say "Thank You"

2. Say It Again

3. Watch What Happens

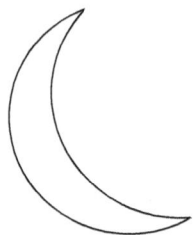

🌀 World Peace

World peace is even more possible than it was yesterday. If we want to see it, we do.

- Create it
- Talk about it
- Watch for it on television
- Listen for it on the radio
- Hunt for it in the newspaper

Instead of fearing our neighbors near and far, we see differences as a blessing and not a curse.

How To Find Peace

We find peace by allowing other people to be who they are, make their own choices, eat the food they want, express themselves how they want, worship who they want, and drive how they want.

Imposing our way or the highway on other people only makes us miserable. What is the point?

If peace is what we seek, we either spend time with peaceful people, in peaceful places, or the complete opposite. Conflict can quickly bring clarity.

There are endless opportunities to practice peace in our lives, if we choose to allow the overwhelming amount of inclusive truths to shine through.

How To Lose Peace

Peace is the opposite of war. Who says peace is right and war is wrong? Of course, it seems people enjoy fighting more than cooperating, but does this make war right? Or peace wrong?

Absolutes in all things lead to either hypocrisy or murder. Clarity and compassion at either extreme do not exist, and are not ever found at either end.

We lose peace when we are unable to let go of our mistakes or the mistakes of others, which are really how we learn about life; at our own speed.

The people in our dreams are aspects of ourselves. When we meet these same people during the day, we remember they too are reflections and will mirror to us our own unresolved issues as long as we have not healed and accepted ourselves the way we are.

The Flip Side Of Peace

Opposites are both the cause and effect of existence; war and peace will dance to and fro our whole lives.

Questions For Reflection

- Are you more inclined towards war or peace?
- What makes you think either is right or wrong?
- Do you allow people to express their views?

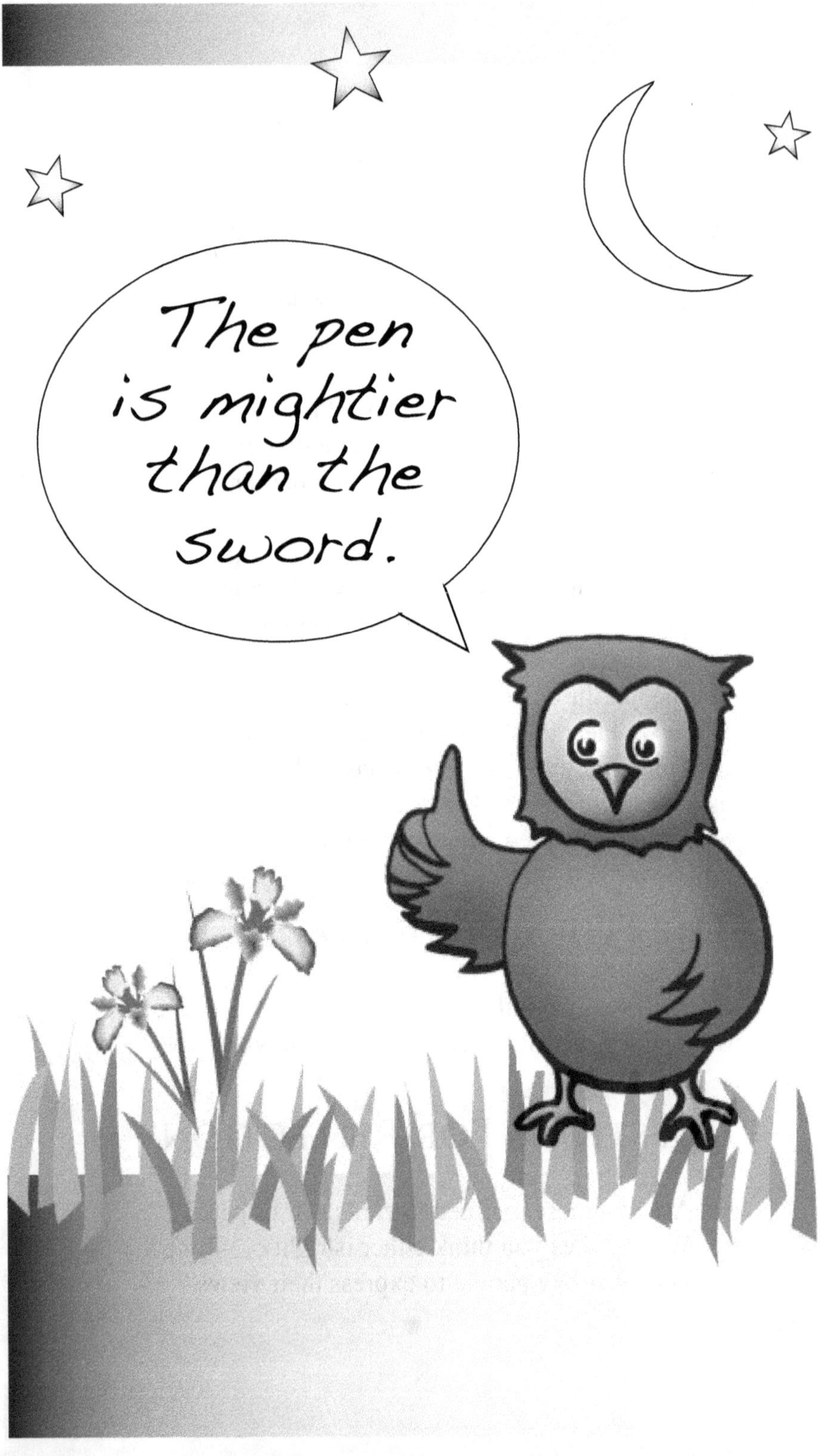
The pen is mightier than the sword.

SANDY'S STORY

I met Sandy on a plane to her country where military service was mandatory. Everyone in her family had, or would, serve their country at home or abroad.

When war broke out with a neighboring nation, Sandy was recruited, naturally followed suit, and was strongly affected by her experiences. She was in her early forties when she was seduced by the anti-war/pro-peace rallies in her city.

So convinced of the validity of her beliefs, Sandy lost it on someone pushing *their* strong views on her and it took an arrest to bring her back to center.

Of course, having spent so much time at one end of the spectrum, she was bound to get a taste of the other. As soon as she recognized her shadow, she was able to accept the opinions of other people, regardless of what they believed.

3 STEPS TO PEACE

1. You Win. They Lose

2. How Does That Feel?

3. No One Wins And No One Loses

🎄 RESOURCES

Now we understand *The Law of Reaction* and how to make it work for us, instead of against us.

We see our reflections only by exposing our shadows; life itself cannot help but mirror our alternating struggles and successes.

Knowing how everything happens is helpful. How can we know happiness without sadness? Life is for living and learning, loving and hating, standing and falling, in case we had not noticed.

So now we know the steps; how about a dance?

WE LEARN BY REPETITION

- We read *The Law of Reaction* again.

- We make notes on the side and make it our book, underlining and highlighting passages we like.

- We re-read our underlines, highlights and notes and learn faster than if we just read the book once and put it on the shelf.

- We prioritize 3 things we want to learn; if we hear something, we forget; if we see something, we remember; if we do something, we understand.

QUESTIONS & ANSWERS

Michael Losier believes people can decide what they want by deciding what they do not want. I often use this perspective and helpful technique to answer my own questions about *The Law of Reaction*.

How can we use *The Law of Reaction* to feel safe walking down the street at night?

By learning self-defence, we are more likely to encounter the thing we wish to defend against, so awareness protects us in the dojo and on the street.

How can we use *The Law of Reaction* to make our lives easier and not so hard?

By letting go of our expectations for specific outcomes. What we want may not serve us, but give us what we need in the perfect amount.

How can we use *The Law of Reaction* to get more free time and take a holiday once in a while?

When our days become filled with tasks, hobbies, meetings, activities and parties, we take a break.

What if we try everything *The Law of Reaction* suggests and still do not see the results we want?

Doing the same things over and over again yet expecting different results drives us nuts. Let's stop!

How can we use *The Law of Reaction* to start our own businesses?

By finding a mentor to teach us what we want to learn, we are exposed to opportunities where learning and earning are connected; success brings equal stress.

How do we use *The Law of Reaction* to attract the right husband/wife/lover/friend/partner?

When contrast has brought clarity, we try a new approach. We go against the grain and be ourselves, if we can; the universe cannot help but balance us.

How can we use *The Law of Reaction* to get a new mini-van/pick-up truck/SUV/sports car?

When our clunkers bite the dust, we do what has to be done. We get a new ride and look after it.

How can we use *The Law of Reaction* to be happy and enjoy our lives?

Learning how everything happens brings a sense of serenity and calm that outlasts anything else.

How can we use *The Law of Reaction* to make more money?

We can give away every cent, or understand we are rewarded in direct proportion to the value we create.

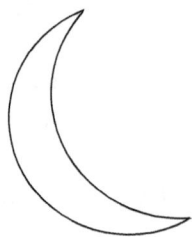

How can we use *The Law of Reaction* to have a baby and start a family?

By harmonizing our health with the natural cycles of our environment and releasing our expectations, we may paradoxically find ourselves expecting.

How can we use *The Law of Reaction* to be good upstanding citizens and contribute to society?

We can drain our community, or contribute our time, money and energy in our own unique ways.

How can we use *The Law of Reaction* to do our homework and pass our exams?

Oscar Wilde said *anything worth knowing cannot be taught*. When we choose a path we choose that path.

How can we use *The Law of Reaction* to plant a garden and harvest some organic food?

We can spend too much time, money and energy on old, wilted, over-priced malnutrition, or begin looking after ourselves by growing food not lawns.

How can we use *The Law of Reaction* to write a book or screenplay?

We read books, watch movies, go to conferences and award shows, get jealous, inspired, or both. Effort equals results with both similar and opposite effects.

Every advance is preceded by a setback.

How can we use *The Law of Reaction* to get our songs on the radio?

We listen to the same songs on the radio long enough to do whatever it takes to get ours over-played too.

How can we use *The Law of Reaction* to tolerate time with our parents/siblings at Christmas?

Wayne Dyer says *what we want from our parents is what we came to give them,* so we celebrate our families every Christmas, until we learn this lesson.

How can we use *The Law of Reaction* to make different choices in our lives?

We make deliberate choices and pay attention to the results. We have to stop lying to ourselves.

How can we use *The Law of Reaction* to reconnect with our ex-wife/husband/partner/lover?

In private, we hate them until we love them, but stay out of their way. No one ruffles our feathers again.

How can we use *The Law of Reaction* to cure ourselves of whatever ill is ailing us?

Funny, near-death experiences almost always seem to get us pointed in the right direction. Our bodies heal themselves, and there is no limit to how long we can live and how much love we can give.

TRY THIS AT HOME

By practicing these exercises in the comfort of our own homes, we have a lot more fun.

If and when we find ourselves accusing someone of something they did or did not do, something they said or did not say, or even something we thought they either did or did not think, we practice accusing them, but say our own name at the end of the sentence.

If your name is Jane, you would say:

"You are so _____, Jane."

If this is difficult, we try the same exercise while looking into a mirror, but imagine ourselves addressing the person with whom we have issue.

Everything we say to some one else, we are actually saying to ourselves, to our shadows, and are using our friends and family members as mirrors.

When we listen to how we talk to people, we can learn all about ourselves. We use these clues to solve the case of why our life is, or is not, working the way we want it to.

Of course, the flip side is true too. We cannot take anything personally. When someone is talking to us, remember they are talking to themselves, especially when they are praising or criticizing us.

Other people will do and say and think whatever they want to. Nothing we do will ever change that.

Every single person in our lives is a teacher. We can learn anything we ever wanted to know about ourselves, simply by listening to how we talk to other people, and by hearing the thoughts we think.

Instead of saying the words *good* or *bad,* say *that's different.* This shifts our perspective from labelling other people, when we are really labeling ourselves. This shows us what we truly believe.

When we are convinced without a doubt in the world that someone or something is a certain way, the opposite will always be true too. Our shadows are our best teachers, and lurking around with them behind the scenes can lead us to untold riches.

MORE INSPIRATION

- The Alchemist - Paulo Coelho
- Power of Intention - Wayne Dyer
- The Vein of Gold - Julia Cameron
- In Her Own Words - Peace Pilgrim
- Creative Visualization - Shakti Gawain
- The Law of Attraction - Michael Losier
- Way of The Peaceful Warrior - Dan Millman
- Dark Side of The Light Chasers - Debbie Ford
- Survival Into The 21st Century - V. Kulvinskas
- The Monk Who Sold His Ferrari - Robin Sharma
- Lazy Person's Guide To Success - Ernie Zelinski

CONNECTIONS

I enjoy talking about the subject of this book with whomever has something to say about it. If you would like to share your thoughts, send me an email: oliverlukedelorie@gmail.com

ABOUT THE AUTHOR

Oliver Luke Delorie explored both the physical and metaphysical world, before finding his balance in creating and publishing educational multimedia.

GRATITUDE

Thank you for reading *The Law of Reaction*.

This book exists because I saw myself in Antonia Partridge, Michael Losier, Bones Colenbrander, Wayne Dyer, Ernie Zelinski, Tim Ewanchuk, Rick Frishman, James Malinchak, Robin Crow, John Demartini, Shakti Gawain, Paulo Coelho, Fred Alan Wolf, Sacha Levin, Sean Brereton, John Assaraf, Susan Lee, Frederik Ferdinand, Shannen Kennedy, John Fraser, Morris Kaplan, Darrin Caruso, Tanya Pauls, Alex Dedovic, David Gray, Mignon & Keith Lundmark, Debbie Ford, Sarah Binab, Paul Meier, Bob Proctor, Robin Elliott, Byron Katie, Lisette Cook, Beverly Siller, Adriane Enns, Reid Tracy, Robin Steffanick, Gabrielle Levin, Damon Bell, Jason Hudgins and Cindy Lee Yelland.

And last but not least, props to the place where

Two Equals One

This is where, why and how everything happens.

☆

9 780973 591835